J.K. ROWLING

A Real-Life Reader Biography

Ann Gaines

Mitchell Lane Publishers, Inc.
P.O. Box 619
Bear, Delaware 19701

Mitchell Lane
PUBLISHERS

First Printing

Real-Life Reader Biographies

Paula Abdul	Mary Joe Fernandez	Ricky Martin	Arnold Schwarzenegger
Christina Aguilera	Andres Galarraga	Mark McGwire	Selena
Marc Anthony	Sarah Michelle Gellar	Alyssa Milano	Maurice Sendak
Drew Barrymore	Jeff Gordon	Mandy Moore	Dr. Seuss
Brandy	Mia Hamm	Chuck Norris	Shakira
Garth Brooks	Melissa Joan Hart	Tommy Nuñez	Alicia Silverstone
Kobe Bryant	Jennifer Love Hewitt	Rosie O'Donnell	Jessica Simpson
Sandra Bullock	Faith Hill	Rafael Palmeiro	Sinbad
Mariah Carey	Hollywood Hogan	Gary Paulsen	Jimmy Smits
Cesar Chavez	Katie Holmes	Freddie Prinze, Jr.	Sammy Sosa
Christopher Paul Curtis	Enrique Iglesias	Julia Roberts	Britney Spears
Roald Dahl	Derek Jeter	Robert Rodriguez	Sheryl Swoopes
Oscar De La Hoya	Steve Jobs	**J.K. Rowling**	Shania Twain
Trent Dimas	Michelle Kwan	Keri Russell	Liv Tyler
Celine Dion	Bruce Lee	Winona Ryder	Robin Williams
Sheila E.	Jennifer Lopez	Cristina Saralegui	Vanessa Williams
Gloria Estefan	Cheech Marin		Tiger Woods

Library of Congress Cataloging-in-Publication Data
Gaines, Ann.
  J.K. Rowling/Ann Gaines.
    p.cm. — (A real-life reader biography)
  Includes index.
  ISBN 1-58415-078-5
  1. Rowling, J. K.—Juvenile literature. 2. Authors, English—20th century—Biography—Juvenile literature. 3. Potter, Harry (Fictitious character)—Juvenile literature. 4. Children's stories—Authorship—Juvenile literature. [1. Rowling, J.K. 2. Authors, English. 3. Women, Biography.] I. Title. II. Series.
  PR6068.O93 Z67 2001
  823'914—dc21
  [B]   2001029307

ABOUT THE AUTHOR: Ann Graham Gaines holds graduate degrees in American Civilization and Library and Information Science from the University of Texas at Austin. She has been a freelance writer for 18 years, specializing in nonfiction for children. She lives near Gonzales, Texas with her husband and their four children.

PHOTO CREDITS: cover: Archive Photos; p. 4 Globe Photos; p. 6 Globe Photos; p. 8 Globe Photos; p. 20 Corbis; p.28 Globe Photos; p. 30 Archive Photos.
ACKNOWLEDGMENTS: The following story has been thoroughly researched, and to the best of our knowledge, represents a true story. While every possible effort has been made to ensure accuracy, the publisher will not assume liability for damages caused by inaccuracies in the data, and makes no warranty on the accuracy of the information contained herein. This story has not been authorized nor endorsed by J.K. Rowling.

Table of Contents

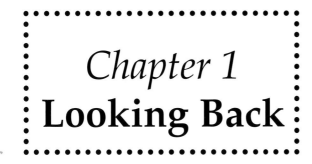

Chapter 1
Looking Back

On July 8, 2000, lots of children and even their parents stayed up well past their bedtimes. Why? Because the fourth Harry Potter book, *Harry Potter and the Goblet of Fire*, went on sale in bookstores at midnight. Thousands of fans had been eagerly waiting for the new book and wanted their copies just as soon as possible.

The book's release made headlines in newspapers and magazines. Television news programs gave it a lot of coverage. So it's not surprising that the first

Thousands of fans eagerly awaited the release of *Harry Potter and the Goblet of Fire.*

printing of hundreds of thousands of copies sold out in a few days.

J.K. Rowling, the author, has become very famous for her books about Harry Potter. Children and grown-ups alike in many different countries have loved the stories she tells about this English orphan. While living with his mean relatives, Harry Potter gets a letter telling him he is a wizard. What a time he will have at Hogwarts

School for Wizards, meeting his professors, making friends, and battling the dark wizard Lord Voldemort!

"I never expected to be in the papers," Rowling said when she was talking to an interviewer about writing her first book, *Harry Potter and the Sorcerer's Stone*. All her life, Rowling had wanted to be a writer. She began writing when she was still just a child. By the time she was 25, she had already written many short stories. She had also written two novels for grown-ups but decided they were not good enough to show to a publisher.

When the idea of a boy arriving for the first time at wizards' school suddenly came to her, Rowling loved it. But to finish *Harry Potter and the Sorcerer's Stone* was a struggle that would take her four full years. She remembers feeling pleased when her literary agent, a person who represents authors and helps them find publishers, called her to say Bloomsbury Press had offered to buy the book. They offered

J.K. Rowling has become very famous for her books about Harry Potter.

her just a few thousand dollars for the manuscript, but that made her perfectly happy. Today, of course, she makes much more money for the books she writes.

This is the story of J.K. Rowling's rise to fame and fortune.

Jo traveled all over the world to promote her books on Harry Potter. Here she is with some children to celebrate her fourth title, Harry Potter & The Goblet of Fire.

Chapter 2
Growing Up

J.K. Rowling's full name is Joanne Kathleen Rowling. She was born on July 31, 1965. When she was a kid, she went by the name Jo—she remembers that when someone called her "Joanne," she knew she was in trouble. Today Jo is still the name she likes to be called.

Her parents were Peter and Ann Rowling. When Jo was born, they lived in the small town of Chipping Sodbury, which is near Bristol, a large industrial city in England. Peter had always liked machines and mechanics. He had been manager of a company that

J.K. Rowling's full name is Joanne Kathleen Rowling. She likes to be called Jo.

manufactured airplanes when he met Ann, who worked in a laboratory where scientific research is performed. Both of them really loved to read.

Growing up, both Peter and Ann Rowling had lived in large cities. But neither one liked the crowds they found there. So after they married, they chose to live in small towns in the country. They liked to roam about the countryside in their free time. They visited larger cities only for special occasions such as shopping trips.

Peter and Ann devoted themselves to Jo as soon as she was born. In 1967, the family expanded to include Joanne's only sibling, a sister named Diane, whom Jo nicknamed Di. The parents would often read aloud to their girls.

From the time she was very small, Jo was a smart and friendly girl. Whether she was by herself, with Di, or playing outside with friends, Jo used her imagination to make up lots of games of "let's pretend." She liked to play that she was all sorts of different people,

Jo has one sister named Diane.

including characters she knew from books.

When Jo was 5, she started to tell Di a long series of stories about rabbits because both of them wanted to have a bunny as a pet. Using her imagination, she created a story about Di falling down a hole and being rescued by a family of rabbits, who fed her strawberries to cheer her up.

At age 6, the usual age for British children, Jo Rowling started school. As soon as she learned to read, she started to write down her own stories. The first one featured Rabbit. This time he came down with the measles. Many visitors came to visit him in his burrow, including one named Miss Bee, whom Rowling would always feel proud of inventing. When she got a little older, she wrote a mystery she called *The Seven Cursed Diamonds*.

All through school, she loved to read and write. Asked as a grown-up to name her favorite authors when she was a child, she immediately named Paul

When they were little, Jo would make up all sorts of stories to tell Diane.

Gallico, Noel Streatfield, E. Nesbit, and C.S. Lewis. As she later would, they all wrote very imaginative stories. Lewis, for example, created a whole different world in his series of books about Narnia.

When she got older, she went to a school called Wyedean Comprehensive. This was like an American high school. She has said her teenage years were painful in some ways, just as they are for many people. She felt shy around older kids and embarrassed about her looks, which she considered plain.

But she always achieved good grades, especially in her literature and foreign language classes. Her last year she was named Head Girl, which meant that she represented the school when important visitors came. She also discovered a new favorite author during these years, a woman named Jessica Mitford. She found Mitford's own life as interesting as her books because she went to Spain to fight in a civil war as a young woman of 19.

As soon as she learned to write, Jo wrote down the stories she made up.

When she graduated from Wyedean, Jo would have liked to become a writer. But she did not know how to go about getting her stories and the novels she hoped to write published. So instead she listened to her parents, who were concerned that she find a way to earn a living. They suggested she go to college and study to become a bilingual secretary, a person who can read and write in two languages. She enrolled at Exeter University and majored in French and literature.

Jo Rowling enjoyed college. She had a boyfriend she really liked. During her third year at Exeter the university sent her to study at a school in Paris, France. She loved living there. The following year she graduated from Exeter and headed out on her own.

When she graduated from high school, she would have liked to become a writer. But she did not know how to get her stories published.

Chapter 3
On Her Own

> **After Jo got out of college, she went from one job to another.**

In the years following college, Jo Rowling did not know quite what to do. She never followed her parents' suggestion that she become a bilingual secretary for a big international company. Instead, she took one job after another. Sometimes she just got bored with a job after a time, and quit. In a couple of cases, she was fired from her job. She readily admits she rarely gave her all to her work. This was because she really wanted to be doing something else.

As she had since childhood, she was dreaming of becoming a writer. She continued to write constantly in her free time. She was often distracted while on the job, thinking about her stories. Sometimes she would even use computers while at work to type up her stories instead of doing the company's business.

During these years, she wrote many short stories and two novels for grown-ups. But she still did not feel ready to try to have anything published. Re-reading her old novels today she thinks she was right—she sees they aren't very good. But she does not regret the time she devoted to writing them. She believes that she later succeeded as a writer largely because she got so much practice writing.

For a time, she lived in London but took a train to a job at the Manchester Chamber of Commerce. She did this even though the trip took her hours, because she was dating someone in Manchester. She was looking out the train window while she was returning home from work one evening when she

She continued to dream about being a writer.

During one of her long train rides, the idea of Harry and Hogwarts just popped into her head.

had a sudden inspiration. In one interview she described it like this: "I suddenly had this basic idea of a boy who didn't know what he was."

She thought then of him receiving the notice that he was to go to wizard school. In another interview she said, "The idea of Harry and Hogwarts just popped into my head. I spent four hours thinking about what Hogwarts would be like—this made it the most interesting train journey I've ever taken. By the time I got off at King's Cross Station, many of the characters in the book had already been invented."

Chapter 4
Harry Potter Grows

After Rowling thought of the character of Harry Potter, she put a lot of time into working on his story. Soon she had made up the terrible family he lives with, the Dursleys. She had decided that they would be Muggles, or humans who have no wizard powers. Then she decided how he became an orphan. When he was a tiny baby, Harry's parents were killed in a terrible battle with a dark wizard. Harry was at this battle, from which he emerged with a scar on his forehead in the shape of a lightning bolt.

Jo spent many hours working on the character of Harry Potter.

Some of the charcters in her book are based loosely on people she once knew.

She invented his best friends. One is a girl named Hermione Granger whom Rowling has said resembles herself at 11, "though I was neither as clever nor as annoying, I hope!" The other is a boy named Ron Weasley, whose entire family would come to love and watch out for Harry.

Rowling also developed the character who would be his worst enemy at school, the snooty Draco Malfoy. She came up with the teachers at Hogwarts, including the wise and wonderful Professor Dumbledore, who runs the school. She has admitted that the professors Harry does not like are loosely based on teachers she once knew.

And she finally decided on the houses' names at Hogwarts while she was taking a trip in an airplane. Because there wasn't any other paper handy, she wrote those names on an airsickness bag.

As she got more and more excited about the book, she entered into a happy time in her life. But it would not last very long because her mother was diagnosed with multiple sclerosis, a terrible disease. Ann Rowling died less than a year later. To this day, Jo Rowling feels badly because she was not at her mother's side when she died.

In the months that followed her mother's death, her daughter grieved. She became depressed and lost her job because more than ever she could not concentrate on her work. But she did not forget about Harry Potter. She continued to think about him and make notes for herself about Harry, Hogwarts, and the story she was creating.

In September 1990, she decided it might do her good to change scenery and leave England for a time. She applied for a job teaching English at a school in Portugal. When she got the news she could have the job, she felt both excited and afraid. But she followed through. She took her notebooks filled with ideas, names, and

In 1990, Jo took a job teaching English at a school in Portugal.

Even after J.K. Rowling came up with the idea of Harry Potter, the wizard, it took her four more years to finish her story and find a publisher for it.

little bits of stories about Harry with her to Portugal.

She filled one whole notebook with notes concerning Quidditch, the ball game Harry loves to play at school. She'd made up the game one night in a hotel room in Manchester. "I wanted a sport for wizards and I'd always wanted to see a game where there was more than one ball in play at the same time," she said. She remembers trying out lots of different names for the balls before she settled on Snitch, Bludgers, and Quaffle.

In Portugal, Rowling lived in a lovely apartment in Oporto, near the school where she taught. She got along well with her students. Her happiness slowly returned as she enjoyed getting to know a beautiful new place. She grew even happier when she met a man and got married. The first two years of their marriage were quite happy, even though her husband's job meant he was extremely busy and often away for days at a time.

But she did not forget about Harry Potter. She continued to fill notebooks with stories about him.

In 1993, Jo gave birth to a daughter she named Jessica.

Rowling continued both to teach and work in her free time on the Harry Potter book. In 1992, she became pregnant. Unfortunately, during her pregnancy, her husband's job as a TV reporter would not let him spend more time with her. She suffered from loneliness and began to be plagued by fits of depression. In 1993, their daughter Jessica was born. Soon after that, Jo Rowling and her husband divorced. She has never said much more about what happened, not even revealing his name, because she wants to keep that phase of her life as private as possible.

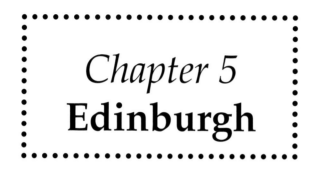

Chapter 5
Edinburgh

After her divorce, Jo Rowling decided to return home to Great Britain. By then, her sister Di was living in Edinburgh, the capital of Scotland. Di asked Jo to come live in Edinburgh so they could be close.

Rowling arrived in Edinburgh with three chapters of *Harry Potter and the Sorcerer's Stone* and notebooks with many more ideas in her bags. At first, she thought she would spend some time with Di and then head back to London. She knew it would be hard for her to find a job in Edinburgh that would make enough money to live on and send

After her divorce, Jo moved to Scotland to be near her sister, Di.

Jessica to day care. Perhaps she could find a better paying job in London.

But one day soon before she planned to leave, Jo decided to take a risk and tell Di about Harry Potter. Up to this point, he had been her secret. When she started to spin the tale, Di liked it and laughed hard, delighting her big sister. Di insisted on reading the rest of what Jo had so far. When she liked that, too, Jo decided she give herself a year to push through and finish the book. She went on welfare, or what is called the dole in Britain. She worked part-time, too. She would also receive a grant from an arts council to work on her book. Altogether she made just enough money to live on.

She and the baby lived in a shabby apartment. Every day, Jo would take Jessica out on a long walk. Once the baby fell asleep, she knew she would have a couple of hours of quiet and they would head for a cafe or coffee shop, where Jo would rock her baby's carriage

It was difficult for her to work with a young child.

and write more *Harry Potter and the Sorcerer's Stone* in longhand.

This was a difficult year, but Jo kept her goal firmly in mind and did, in fact, finish her novel in the time she had allotted herself. Looking back, she says she feels pride in what she did. When her book was completed, she went to the library and looked up names of literary agents. She sent it off to two, hoping one would be willing to represent her and try to sell her book to a publisher. Then she went back to teaching. Jessica was big enough by that time to go to nursery school.

One of the agents soon wrote back to Jo, saying he would like to help her sell her novel. But for a long time, it seemed like Harry Potter might not ever appear in print. The agent sent it out to publisher after publisher. One after another, they wrote back rejecting the book, saying they did not want it. Finally, Bloomsbury Press offered Rowling a few thousand dollars for the book. She was tickled.

By the time Jessica was old enough to go to nursery school, Jo was ready to send Harry Potter to be published.

Her first book about Harry Potter was sold to Bloomsbury Press for a few thousand dollars.

Then, in 1997, she received even more exciting news. Even though *Harry and the Sorcerer's Stone* had not yet appeared in print, word of the book had spread beyond Bloomsbury. Every year a big book fair is held in Bologna, Italy. European publishers show off their new books there. But something else happens there, too. Publishers auction off the foreign rights to their books—in other words, British publishers sell American publishers the right to print one of their titles.

That year Jo Rowling's book was the one that excited the most interest. Unknown to her, bidding was fast and furious. Arthur Levine of Scholastic Press put in the winning bid of $100,000 for Harry Potter. This made publishing history. Never before had anyone paid so much for the right to publish a children's book.

Chapter 6
Fame and Fortune

Harry Potter would be a phenomenon, the likes of which J.K. Rowling and the publishing world had never dreamed. Asked about whether she had expected success, she said, "Never. I just wrote the sort of thing I liked reading. I didn't expect lots of people to like them, in fact, I never really thought much past getting them published." But Harry Potter was very popular first in England and then in the United States and elsewhere in the world.

Rowling's first book received excellent reviews and made best-seller

Her first book received great reviews and made the best-seller lists in England.

Children all over the world love to dress up like Harry Potter. Jo visits and talks to many kids.

lists. She also received many important awards for it, including Great Britain's National Book Award. It appeared on many lists of the best books published in 1998. Jo Rowling herself was the subject of many articles in magazines. She became famous.

What would happen next? Could J.K. Rowling repeat her success and write another great book? She had already

considered this problem. Rowling had gotten nervous after she turned the first book in, while she was waiting for it to appear in print. It can take months for a book to appear after a publisher buys it.

But instead of letting fear overcome her, she faced her problem head-on by sitting down and working out the plots for a series of seven books. She decided each one would cover one of Harry's years at Hogwarts and outlined basically what would happen in each. The series will end when he graduates from Hogwarts and goes off to find his own way in the world. She has said she knows what each book needs: humor, strong characters, a very tight plot, and scariness. Bloomsbury and Scholastic signed contracts with her for the entire series.

Soon, her books were sold all over the world. She became very famous.

The appearance of numbers two, three, and four—*Harry Potter and the Chamber of Secrets, Harry Potter and the Prison of Azkaban,* and *Harry Potter and the Goblet of Fire* —met the publishers' expectations. Their popularity increased

At the annual Easter Egg Roll at the White House on April 24, 2000, J.K. Rowling read from her Harry Potter books on the White House lawn.

to such an extent that news reports talked about the "Harry Potter craze." Critics continued to praise the books. Teachers expressed appreciation to J.K. Rowling for creating an enormous interest in reading. Fans rejoiced when the news appeared that the first book was going to be made into a movie, scheduled for release in November 2001.

Today Jo Rowling still likes to read in her free time. Jane Austen is her favorite author. When she is working, she

spends most of her time writing, but she also goes out to promote her books. On a book tour in Canada, she read to a crowd of 15,000 that turned up to see her at a sports arena.

But she thinks the most important thing she does is raise her daughter. She points out that being a single parent is hard even if you're rich and famous. She is devoted to Jessica, who often travels with her. They continue to live in Edinburgh.

Reflecting on her life, she has said, "If someone asked for my recipe for happiness, step one would be finding out what you love doing most in the world and step two would be finding someone to pay you to do it. I consider myself very lucky indeed to be able to support myself by writing."

In the future she thinks she might try to write a book for adults, but that depends on what new ideas come to her. It seems likely they'll be amazing. Readers all over the world can hardly wait.

Despite all her success, Jo still thinks the most important thing she does each day is raise her daughter, Jessica.

Chronology

- 1965, born on July 31.
- 1967, birth of Diane, her only sibling.
- 1971, starts school at age 6. When she learns to read, she will begin to write down the stories she loves to make up.
- 1984, leaves home to attend Exeter University.
- 1988, graduates from college and starts a series of jobs that mean little to her while dreaming of becoming a writer.
- 1990, moves to Portugal after her mother's death and finds a job teaching English.
- 1993, gives birth to daughter Jessica but soon divorces her husband. She and Jessica return to Great Britain.
- 1994, finishes writing *Harry Potter and the Sorcerer's Stone*.
- 1997, makes publishing history when Arthur Levine of Scholastic Press pays $100,000 for the rights to publish *Harry Potter and the Sorcerer's Stone* in the United States.
- 2000, releases fourth book, *Harry Potter and the Goblet of Fire*, which goes on sale at midnight on July 8 as thousands of fans stay up to get their copies.

Index